Aidan Meehan was born in Northern Ireland, and educated in Newry and at Queen's University, Belfast. After leaving Ireland in 1973, he discovered a deep interest in Celtic art, which led to his eight-volume *Celtic Design Series* and to his *Celtic Patterns for Painting and Crafts*, *Celtic Alphabets* and *Celtic Borders*, also published by Thames & Hudson.

The Book of Kells

Painting Book

Aidan Meehan

Thames & Hudson

artwork and typography
copyright © 1999 Aidan Meehan

First published in the United States of America in
paperback in 1999 by Thames & Hudson Inc.,
500 Fifth Avenue, New York, New York 10110

Library of Congress Catalog Card Number 99-70863

ISBN 0-500-28146-7

Printed and bound in Spain

Contents

6   Introduction

8   Folio 1v : cats and birds

10   Folio 3v : cats

14   Folio 4R : cats and birds

18   Folio 5R : men, birds and cats

26   Folio 7v : cats and men

30   Folio 29R : cats

32   Folio 34R : cats, birds, eels and men

42   Folio 114R : cats

44   Folio 124R : birds

46   Folio 130R : cats, birds, men and eels

52   Folio 133R : men and birds

54   Folio 183R : cats

55   Folio 188R : cats, men, birds and eels

61   Folio 291R : eels

62   Folio 292R : eels

64   Source Books

Introduction

These designs are all ready to paint. You can use coloured pencils, markers, or drawing inks, but they are really meant for painting. Some designs are simpler than others, so practise on these first. Save your favourites, and the more complex ones, until last.

Tempera was the paint used in the Book of Kells. Pigments are mixed with egg yolk or egg white to make tempera colours. These days, it is sold in jars (sometimes labelled "plaka") at artists' suppliers. It also comes in powder form, for mixing with water. Buy "artists' quality" paint, rather than "students' quality".

Designers' gouache (pronounced "gwaash") is like tempera, fast-drying and as easy to use. It is a solid, opaque paint: you can brush one coat over a dry undercoat, the two will not mix. So you can change your mind as you paint. You cannot rework watercolour paint.

Closer to tempera, acrylic is reworkable, but also dries waterproof, so never let it dry in the brush. Clean hardened brushes with alcohol. To make it semi-transparent, mix with clear acrylic medium. You can glaze with this acrylic medium, using a clear coat between two layers of transparent colour. Several layers will produce the effect of glass enamelling.

In the Book of Kells, layers of translucent colours are sandwiched between intervening coats of a clear varnish called glair (pronounced "glar"), a medium of egg white whipped up into a stiff meringue, allowed to sit over night, then strained through a cheese cloth.

You can add a little colour to this glair for very transparent effects. To apply glaze as in the Book of Kells, first lay a thin wash of yellowed glair over the drawing. Let it dry, then coat with clear varnish. When dry, lay a second colour on top of the glaze, such as a thin pink over yellow to make orange: light passes through the layers, reflects off the paper and bounces back out, making the colours appear to glow from within. If you feel that glair is too much bother to make, clear acrylic matte medium is just as effective.

Paint bright, light colours inside the bodies, contrasting with dark neutral colours in the background, such as brown or a warm black. A drop of red added to black will warm it to approximate the original oak gall ink.

The traditional palette is white for cheeks, hands, feet, paws, or nails, and golden yellow for edges of bodies, topknots and tails. Rust red - actually iron oxide - was used, mainly for underpainting. Red lead was also used, but as lead is toxic, it is better to use light vermilion. The green is known as verdigris - copper acetate. This is a pale blue green with a drop of grey in it. The blue was lapis lazuli, for which French ultramarine is now used instead. Finally, red-violet was often mixed with the rust red, and applied thinly as a wash.

Each drawing is numbered with the original folio from which I took the design. If you can find a copy of the Book of Kells, you can compare my drawings with the original pages. I have changed the designs, of course, to fit the purpose of this book, but you should still be able to recognise the original models. You will be amazed to realise just how tiny the original drawings are.

Folio 3v (a)

Folio 3v (b)

Folio 3v (c)   [12]

[13]

Folio 4r (a)   [14]

Folio 4r (b)

Folio 4r (c)   [16]

Folio 4r (d)

Folio 5r (a,1)

Folio 5r (a, 2)

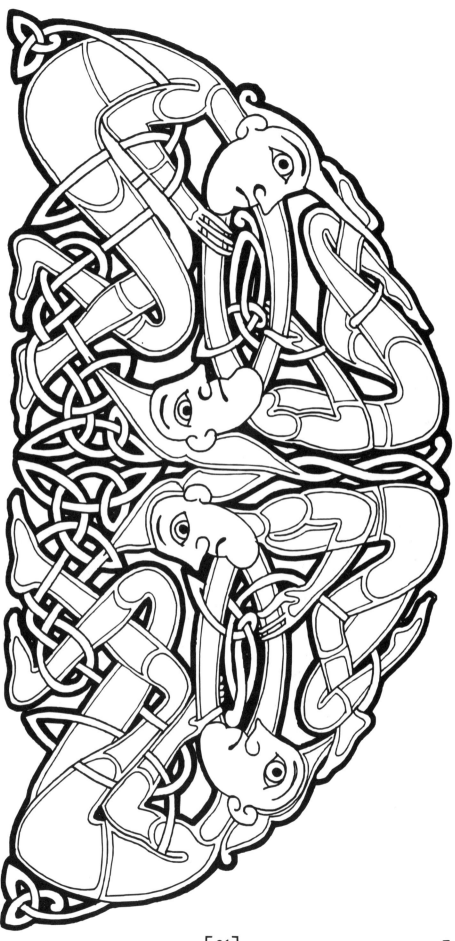

[21]

Folio 5r (c,l)

[22]

Folio 5r (c, 2)

Folio 5r (d,1)

Folio 5r (d, 2)

Folio 7v (a,1)

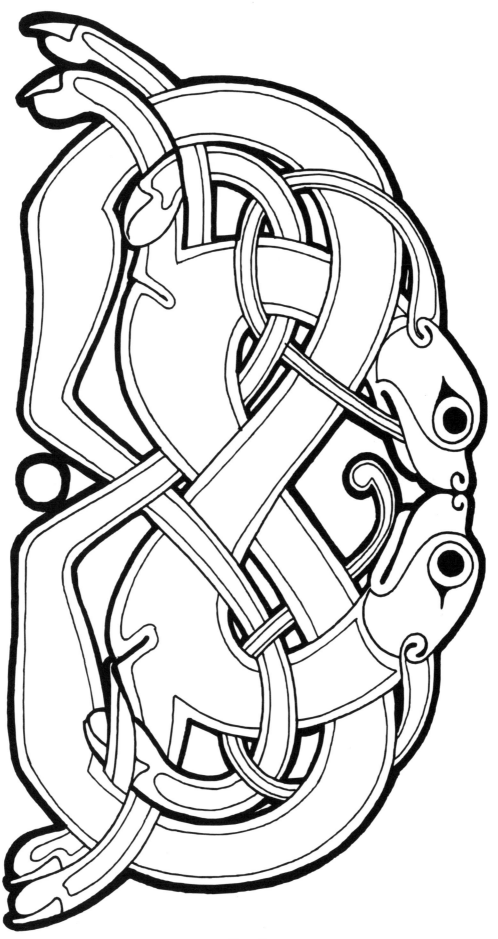

Folío 7v (a, 2)

Folio 7v (c)

Folio 29r (a) [30]

[31]

Folio 34r (a)   [32]

[33]

Folio 34r (c)

Folio 34r (d)

Folio 34r (f)

Folío 34r (h)

Folio 114r (b)

Folio 124r (a)   [44]

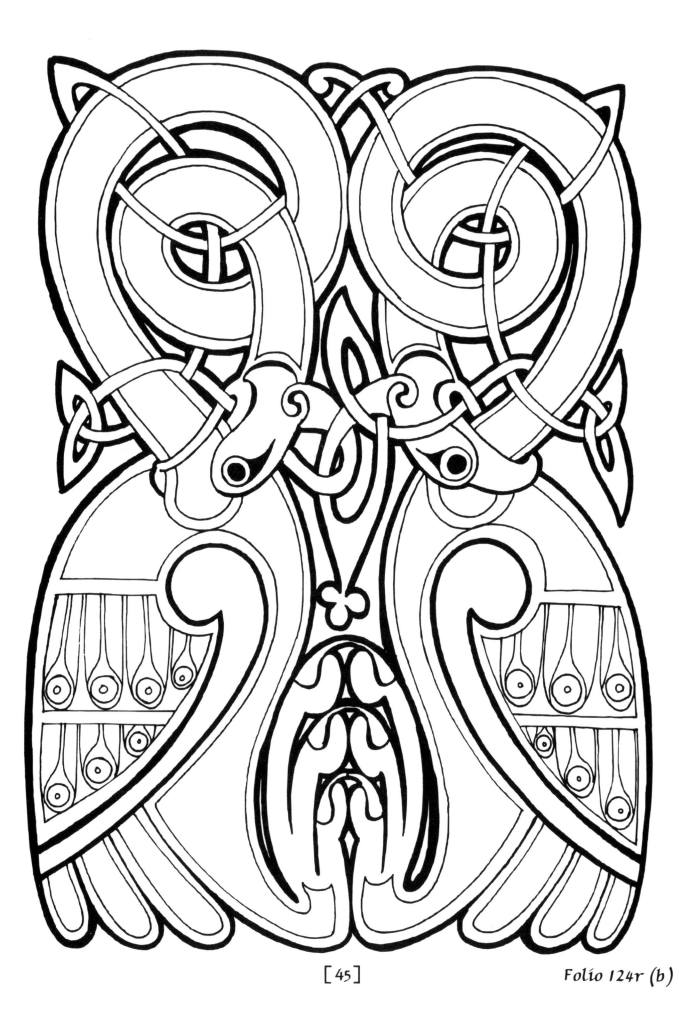

Folio 124r (b)

Folio 130r (b)

Folio 130r (c) [48]

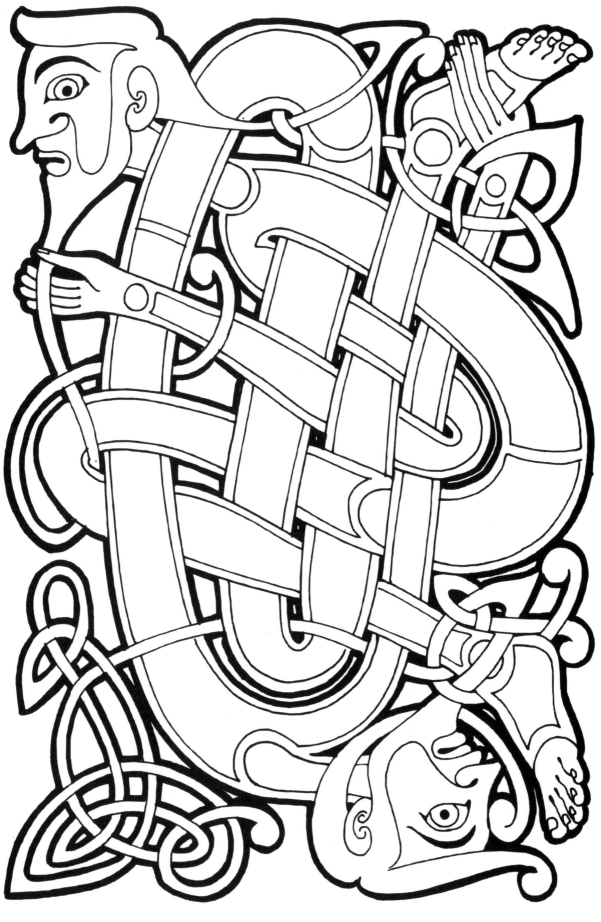

Folio 130r (d)

Folio 130r (e)

Folio 130r (f)

Folio 130r (g) [52]

Folio 133r (b)

Folio 183r (a)   [54]

Folio 188r (a)

Folio 188r (b)   [56]

Folio 188r (c)

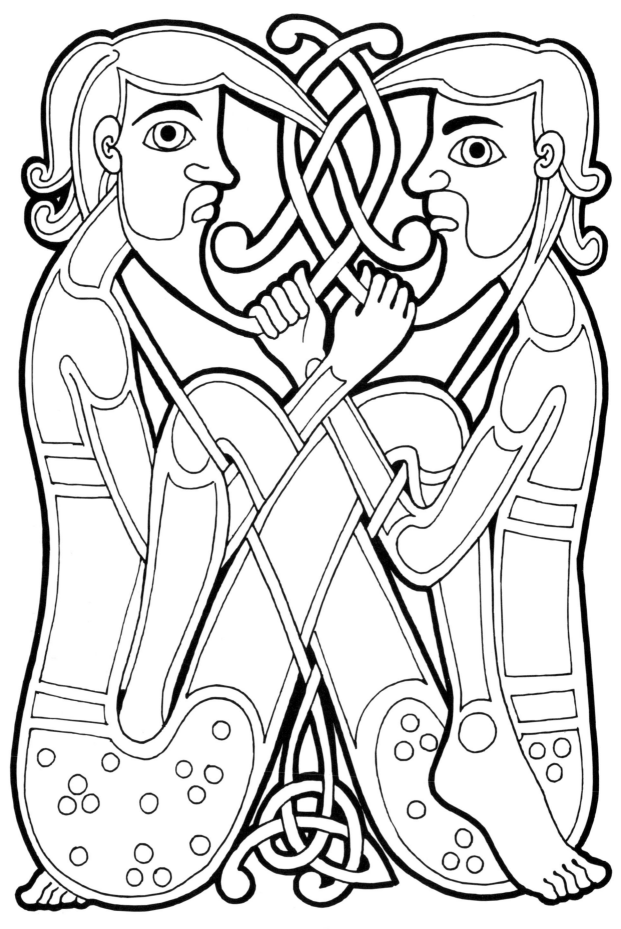

Folio 188r (d)   [58]

Folio 188r (e)

Folio 291r (a)

Folio 292r (a)

Folio 292r (b)

SOURCE BOOKS

Other books by Aidan Meehan with animal patterns from
the Book of Kells similar to those in this book:

Celtic Design: Animal Patterns
Celtic Design: Illuminated Letters

Celtic Patterns Painting Book (the title of the American edition
is Celtic Patterns for Painting and Crafts)

Celtic Alphabets
Celtic Borders

(all published by Thames and Hudson)

Françoise Henry, The Book of Kells, London, 1974
Bernard Meehan, The Book of Kells: an Introduction to the Manuscript
at Trinity College Dublin, London, 1994